For Russell Burgess and the boys of Wandsworth Scho[ol]

WHEN ICICLES HAN[G]

1. ICICLES

*(Shakespeare)

* From *Love's Labour's Lost*

Instrumentation: 2 Fl., 2 Ob., 2 Cl., Bsn., 2 Hns., 2 Tpts., Perc.(2 players), Hp., Strings
For Contents see back cover.

© Oxford University Press 1975

Printed in Great Britain

OXFORD UNIVERSITY PRESS, MUSIC DEPARTMENT, GREAT CLARENDON STREET, OXFORD OX2 6DP
Photocopying this copyright material is ILLEGAL.

When i - ci - cles hang by the wall,

And Dick the shep-herd blows his nail,

And Tom bears logs in-to the hall,

And milk comes fro-zen home in pail,

When blood is nipped, and ways be foul,

Joan doth keel _____ the pot.

doth keel the

When all a - round the wind doth blow, _____ And cough-ing

5

drowns the par-son's saw,
And birds sit brood-ing in the
And birds
snow,
And Ma-rian's nose looks red and raw,
When
sit in the snow,
S.
A.
T.
B.
roa - sted crabs hiss in the bowl,
roa - sted crabs hiss in the bowl,
roa - sted crabs hiss in the bowl,
roa - sted crabs hiss in the bowl,

Then night-ly sings ___ the sta-ring owl, ___ To - wit ___ to -

who! ___ a mer - ry note, ___ While

grea - - sy Joan doth keel ___ the

doth keel the

2. WINTER NIGHTS

(Thomas Campion)

Instrumentation: 2 Fl., 2 Ob., 2 Cl., Bsn., 2 Hn., 2 Perc., Hp., Strings

Now win-ter nights en-large ___ The num-ber of their hours, And clouds their storms dis-charge ___ Up-on the ai-ry towers. Let now the chim - neys blaze ___ And cups ___ o'er-flow ___ with wine: ___

Now yel - low wax - en lights ____ Shall wait on ho -ney love, While youth-ful re - vels, ____ masques, ___ and court- ly sights ____ Sleep's lead- en spells ____ re - move.

This time doth well dis- pense ____ With lo-vers' long dis-course;

Much speech hath some de- fence, ____ Though beau-ty no re- morse. All do not all ___

The sum-mer hath his joys, _____ And win-ter his de-lights; Though love and all his plea-sures are _____ but _____ toys, _____

They short-en te - - dious nights.

Meno mosso

Tempo I

3. GOOD ALE

(15th century)

Instrumentation as for No. 1

Nor bring us in no

T. B.

mp Bring us in good ale, and bring us in good ale,

tripes, — for they be sel-dom clean,

bring us in good ale, and

But bring us in good ale.

bring us in good ale.

Ob.

f

good ale, and bring us in good ale, good ale.

And bring us in good ale.

Cl.

gliss.

mf

20

con spirito ma troppo

Hn.

Bsn.

mf

Bring us in no pud - dings, for

mf

f

gliss.

there-in is all goat's blood; Nor bring us in no ve - ni - son, for that is not for our

4. BLOW, BLOW, THOU WINTER WIND

*(Shakespeare)

*from *As you like it*

Instrumentation: 2 Fl., Hp., Hpschd., Strings

man's in-gra-ti - tude, _____ as man's in - gra - ti -
- tude; _____ Thy tooth is not so keen, _____ Be -
- cause thou art not seen, _____ Al - though thy breath be __
rude, _____ al - though thy breath be rude. _____

32

Attacca
No.5

5. WINTER WAKENETH ALL MY CARE

(14th century)

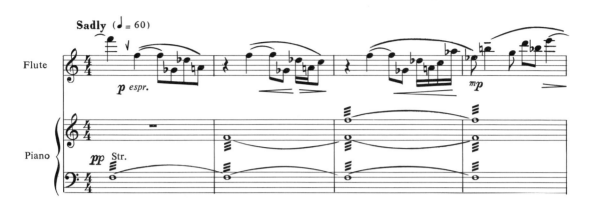

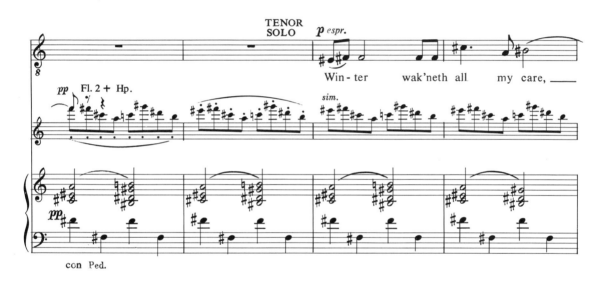

Instrumentation: 2 Fl., 2 Ob., 2 Cl., Bsn., 2 Hn., 2 Perc., Hp., Strings

36

sooth* it is: ___ All go - eth ___ but God - des will.

___ All go - eth ___ but God - des will.

Ww.

dim. _____

All we shall die, ___ though us like ill. ___

(Tempo rubato)

Fl.

marc.

cresc. _____ f

(trem.)

dim. _____ p

(con Ped.)

* sooth = true

* falloweth = withereth

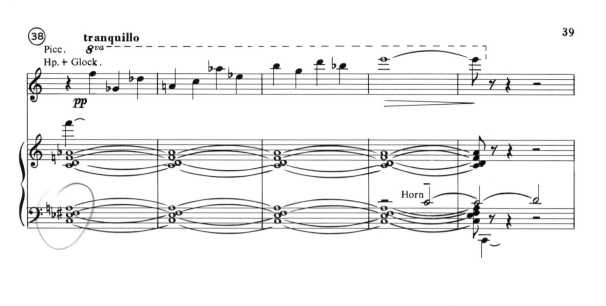

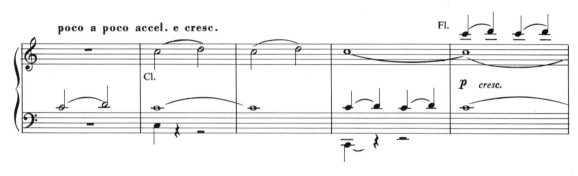

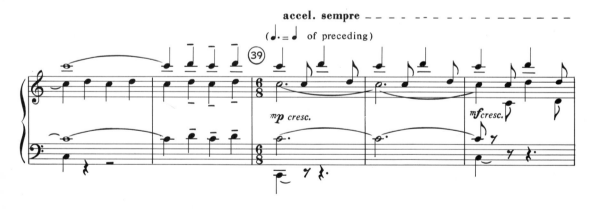

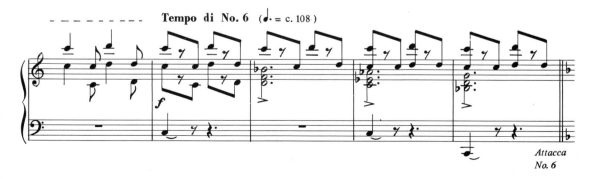

Attacca
No. 6

6. HAY, AY

(Anon., c. 1500)

Instrumentation as for No. 1

* lere = teach

44

Hay, ay, hay, ay;

To dry his clothes till it were day!

ALL VOICES

Mend the fire, and make good cheer!

Fill the cup, Sir Bo-te-lere! Let

ev-'ry man drink to his fere.*

This
Sopr. only

* fere = companion

Reproduced and printed by
Halstan & Co. Ltd., Amersham, Bucks., England